David's Song Of Deliverance Praising God Through Every Storm

Joshua Rhoades

Published by Joshua Paul Rhoades, 2024.

While every precaution has been taken in the preparation of this book, the publisher assumes no responsibility for errors or omissions, or for damages resulting from the use of the information contained herein.

DAVID'S SONG OF DELIVERANCE PRAISING GOD THROUGH EVERY STORM

First edition. September 22, 2024.

Copyright © 2024 Joshua Rhoades.

ISBN: 979-8227033772

Written by Joshua Rhoades.

Also by Joshua Rhoades

Courage Under Fire: David's Stand On The Battlefield
Jonah's Journey: Voices Of Redemption And Lessons In Obedience
The Furnace Of Faith: 12 Principles From The Heat Of Faith
Whispers of Hope: Inspiring Stories of Men's Prayers In Scripture
Frontier Legends: The Oregon Dream
Elijah: A Beacon Of Boldness
HOOK, LINE & SAVIOUR - Faith Reflections from Fishing
Driven By Faith: Motor Racing Inspired Christian Life
30 Day Devotional - Bold and Strong- Coffee Devotions for a Courageous Christian Walk
Authentic Christianity: The Heart of Old Time Religion
Consider The Ant - God's Tiny Preachers
Flee Fornication: The Plea For Purity
Renewed Hope- How to Find Encouragement in God
Sounding The Call - The Voice of Conviction
The Altar - Where Heaven Meets Earth
The Bible's Battlefields- Timeless Lessons from Ancient Wars
The Sacred Art of Silence - How Silence Speaks in Scripture
Under Fire- The Sanctity of the Traditional Biblical Home
Who Is on the Lord's Side? A Call to Righteousness
What Is Truth? - From Skepticism to Submission
First and Goal- Faith and Football Fundamentals
From Dugout to Devotion- Spiritual Lessons from Baseball
Par for the Course- Faith and Fairways
The Believer's Pace- Tools for Running Life's Marathon
The Immutable Fortress- Security in God's Unchanging Nature
Biblical Bravery
Deer Stands and Devotions: A Hunter's Walk with God

Jesus Knows- Our Hearts, Our Responsibility
Restoration - Setting The Bone
Spiritual 911- God's Word for Life's Emergency's
The Freedom of Forgiveness
The Jezebel Effect - Ancient Manipulations Modern Lessons
The Shout That Stopped The Saviour
The Time Machine Chronicles: Old Testament Characters
Anchored In Truth Exploring The Depths of Psalm 119
Biblical Counsel on Anger
Proverbs' Portraits The Men God Mentions
Stumbling in the Dark - The Dangers of Alcohol
Guarding the Wicket Protecting Your Faith and Game
The Champion's Faith - Wrestling and Achieving Spiritual Victory
Scriptural Commands for Modern Times Living God's Word Today Volume 1
Scriptural Commands for Modern Times Living God's Word Today Volume 2
Scriptural Commands for Modern Times Living God's Word TodayVolume3
The Greatest Gift
A Christmas Journey of Faith
Daughter Of The King: Embracing Your Identity In Christ
Determination and Dedication Building Strong Faith As A Young Man
Walking Through Walls God's Power to Part the Storms of Life
David's Song Of Deliverance Praising God Through Every Storm

Dedication

To you, dear reader,

This book, "David's Song of Deliverance: Praising God Through Every Storm" is written with you in mind. Whether you find yourself in a season of peace or in the midst of life's most difficult storms, this journey is for you. Life, much like the story of King David, is filled with moments of triumph, joy, and deep faith, but also with struggles, battles, and heartache. There are times when the weight of your circumstances may seem too heavy to bear, when the world around you feels chaotic, and when your soul is weary. It's in these moments that David's story resonates the most deeply. His life wasn't easy. It was filled with trials that could have easily broken him. But instead of being crushed by the challenges he faced, David found refuge in God, and from that place of safety, his praises rose higher than ever.

This book is dedicated to you because, like David, you are walking a path that may at times seem overwhelming. You may feel surrounded by uncertainty, fear, or discouragement. But just as David discovered, there is a secret to navigating life's storms: praising God through them. When the winds and waves of life threaten to overtake you, the act of lifting your voice in praise becomes your anchor, grounding you in the unwavering truth that God is your deliverer.

You see, David's life is more than just an ancient story of a shepherd-king; it's a blueprint for how we, too, can find strength, comfort, and peace in the most trying of times. This book is not merely a study of David's history; it's an invitation for you to embrace the same spirit of praise and trust that David clung to throughout his life. As you read through the pages, may you find not only the encouragement to praise God in your own storms but also the hope and assurance that He is walking with you, just as He walked with David.

Perhaps you are facing personal trials, emotional struggles, or even spiritual battles that leave you feeling lost or defeated. It is my prayer that through the lessons in David's life and psalms, you will see that you are not alone. David faced his own battles—betrayal, exile, and enemies on every side—yet his faith remained steadfast, not because he had all the answers but because he knew his God was greater than the storms he faced. You, too, can have that same confidence. God's faithfulness to David is the same faithfulness He offers to you today.

This book is dedicated to those who need a reminder that praise is not a mere response to victory but a powerful declaration of faith in the midst of struggle. It's dedicated to those who seek to lift their hearts in worship even when the world seems to be crashing down. It's dedicated to those who want to experience God's deliverance not by escaping their circumstances but by meeting Him in the storm.

So, dear reader, I dedicate this journey to you. May the lessons from David's life inspire you, and may his song of deliverance become your song as well. As you walk through your own storms, may you find the courage to lift your voice in praise and discover that God's deliverance is sure, His presence is near, and His love never fails.

With gratitude and hope,
Joshua Rhoades

Introduction

In the pages of this book, "David's Song of Deliverance: Praising God Through Every Storm", we embark on a journey through the life of one of the Bible's most iconic figures, King David. Known for his unmatched courage, deep faith, and heartfelt psalms, David's life was anything but easy. He faced trials that would leave most people shattered: being hunted by a king who once loved him, living in exile, enduring betrayal, and battling enemies on every side. Yet through it all, David found his refuge in God, and it was in those darkest moments that his praises to the Lord soared the highest. His psalms, especially Psalm 34, reflect a heart that understood that true deliverance comes not from escaping life's storms but from praising God through them.

This book explores how David mastered the art of praising God in every season of life, especially in the midst of adversity. The focus is on how we, too, can learn from David's example. When the world around us is filled with chaos and uncertainty, when we feel surrounded by fear and discouragement, how can we lift our hearts in praise? David's life and psalms provide the blueprint. He didn't shy away from expressing his pain, but in every situation, he returned to one key truth: God is his deliverer. His song of deliverance was one of trust, hope, and relentless praise.

As we journey through the storms of life—whether they come in the form of personal trials, emotional struggles, or spiritual battles—David's example shows us that praise is our anchor. This book will guide you through the many lessons we can learn from David's psalms and life experiences. Through his words, we discover the power of turning our focus away from the storm and onto the One who commands the winds and waves. We will explore how praise invites God's presence, strengthens our faith, and shifts our perspective, allowing us to experience His peace and deliverance in ways we never thought possible.

"David's Song of Deliverance" is more than a study of biblical history; it's a practical guide to living a life of praise, no matter the storms you face. Whether you're dealing with grief, fear, uncertainty, or a season of waiting, this book will encourage you to lift your voice to God. Like David, you can discover the strength, comfort, and deliverance that come from praising God through every storm. This journey will remind you that the God who delivered David is the same God who walks with you today. His faithfulness endures, and His deliverance is sure.

Chapter 1 - Magnifying the Lord

In Psalm 34:3, David says, "O magnify the Lord with me, and let us exalt His name together," which is a powerful statement, especially given the context of his life at that time. David was a man who faced many storms, both literal and figurative, throughout his life. He was pursued relentlessly by King Saul, betrayed by those he trusted, and faced incredible personal challenges. Yet, in the midst of all this, David chose to magnify the Lord rather than focusing on the difficulties surrounding him. This decision to "magnify the Lord" is a profound lesson for us, especially when we encounter our own storms and persecutions. David's example teaches us that when we are going through difficult times—whether it's persecution, betrayal, or personal hardship—our focus should not be on the magnitude of our problems but on the greatness of God. By choosing to magnify the Lord, David made a conscious effort to shift his perspective from the overwhelming nature of his struggles to the incomparable greatness of God.

When David calls us to magnify the Lord, he's not asking us to make God bigger than He already is—God is already infinitely great. Rather, David is encouraging us to change the way we view our circumstances in light of God's power and presence. The word "magnify" means to make something appear larger, and in this context, it's about making God's presence and power seem larger than the trials we are facing. It's about putting our focus on Him rather than on the things that threaten to overwhelm us. David understood this because he lived it. When he was hiding in caves, fleeing from Saul's armies, he could have easily been consumed by fear, anger, and despair. But instead, David chose to magnify the Lord. He didn't deny that his problems were real, but he refused to let those problems be the focus of his attention. By magnifying the Lord, David was declaring that God was bigger than his enemies, bigger than his fears, and bigger than any danger he faced. This is a powerful lesson for us. No matter what storms we face, whether they are external persecutions or internal struggles, we are called to magnify the Lord and exalt His name, recognizing that He is greater than anything we are going through.

Magnifying the Lord in the midst of persecution is not easy, and David's life shows us that this kind of worship is often a deliberate and intentional choice. In the natural, when we are under attack, our instinct is often to focus on the source of our pain or to become consumed by the fear and uncertainty of our situation. David, however, chose a different path. He chose to magnify the Lord, even when his life was in danger. This teaches us that worship and praise are not contingent on our circumstances. David didn't wait for everything to be perfect before he praised God; he praised God in the storm. This is a key lesson for all of us: the time to magnify the Lord is not just when things are going well, but especially when things are difficult. In fact, it is in the midst of persecution and hardship that magnifying the Lord becomes a powerful act of faith. It is a declaration that we trust in God's sovereignty, even when we don't fully understand what is happening around us.

David's call to magnify the Lord also reminds us that worship is a communal act. He says, "Let us exalt His name together." In times of persecution, it is easy to feel isolated and alone, as though no one understands what we are going through. David likely felt this way at times as he fled from Saul and dealt with betrayal from those he trusted. But rather than withdrawing into himself, David invited others to join him in magnifying the Lord. This teaches us that in our storms, we are not meant to go through them alone. There is power in coming together with others to worship and exalt God. When we worship together, we remind each other of God's greatness and faithfulness, which can be especially encouraging during times of persecution. The storms of life can make us feel small and insignificant, but when we gather with others to magnify the Lord, we are reminded of the power and presence of God that transcends our circumstances. Together, we lift our voices in praise, declaring that God is greater than our struggles, and this collective worship strengthens our faith and gives us the courage to persevere.

Another important lesson from David's call to magnify the Lord is that it shifts our focus from ourselves to God. When we are going through persecution or hardship, it's natural to become self-focused, dwelling on our pain, our fear, and our uncertainty. But magnifying the Lord requires us to take our eyes off ourselves and put them on God. This doesn't mean that our problems disappear, but it does mean that our perspective changes. When we magnify God, we are reminded of His greatness, His power, and His faithfulness. We remember that He is in control, even when our lives feel out of control. This shift in focus is crucial because it helps us to see our circumstances in light of who God is, rather than seeing God in light of our circumstances. David's ability to praise God in the midst of persecution shows us that even in our darkest moments, we can find hope and strength when we focus on the greatness of God rather than the size of our problems.

David's life also teaches us that magnifying the Lord in the midst of persecution builds our faith. When David praised God, he wasn't doing so out of denial of his circumstances. He was fully aware of the dangers he faced. But by magnifying the Lord, David was declaring his faith in God's ability to deliver him. This act of worship was a statement of trust—trust that God would see him through the storm, that God was bigger than his enemies, and that God's plans for his life were greater than the threats he faced. Magnifying the Lord in the midst of persecution is an act of faith because it requires us to believe that God is still worthy of our praise, even when life is difficult. It is a way of saying, "I may not understand what's happening, but I know that God is good, and I trust Him to bring me through this."

David's call to magnify the Lord also reveals that worship is a form of spiritual warfare. When David was being pursued by Saul, his life was in constant danger. He was often on the run, hiding in caves, and surrounded by enemies. But instead of giving in to fear or despair, David chose to worship. In doing so, he was engaging in spiritual warfare. Magnifying the Lord in the midst of persecution is a way of standing firm against the enemy. It is a declaration that no matter what the enemy throws at us, we will continue to praise God. This act of worship confounds the enemy because it demonstrates that our hope is not in our circumstances but in God. When we magnify the Lord, we are saying that we will not be shaken by persecution or trials. Instead, we will stand firm in our faith, trusting that God will deliver us.

Moreover, David's call to magnify the Lord teaches us that praise can bring peace in the midst of turmoil. Psalm 34 is filled with expressions of David's trust in God's deliverance, and we see that praising God in the midst of his trials brought him peace. Even though David was facing immense challenges, he found comfort in magnifying the Lord. This is because when we praise God, we are reminded of His presence and His promises. Worshiping God helps us to refocus our minds and hearts on what is true—that God is with us, that He is for us, and that He will never leave us nor forsake us. In times of persecution, it is easy to feel overwhelmed by fear and uncertainty, but praise helps us to anchor ourselves in the unchanging truth of God's character. By magnifying the Lord, David was able to find peace in the midst of persecution, and this is a lesson for all of us. When we face storms in life, whether they are external persecutions or internal struggles, we can find peace by focusing on the greatness of God.

Ultimately, magnifying the Lord in the midst of persecution is about perspective. David's life teaches us that we cannot always control our circumstances, but we can control where we place our focus. By choosing to magnify the Lord, David was able to rise above the fear and uncertainty that surrounded him. He was able to find strength, peace, and hope in the midst of persecution because he chose to focus on God's greatness rather than his own struggles. This is a lesson that we can apply to our own lives. When we face persecution, hardship, or any kind of storm, we have a choice. We can focus on the size of our problems, or we can focus on the greatness of our God. David's call to magnify the Lord reminds us that no matter how big our problems may seem, God is always greater. When we choose to magnify the Lord, we are declaring that we trust in His power, His goodness, and His faithfulness, even when we can't see the way forward.

In conclusion, Psalm 34:3 teaches us the importance of magnifying the Lord in the midst of persecution. David's life is a powerful example of what it means to praise God even when the storms of life are raging. By choosing to focus on God's greatness rather than his own struggles, David was able to find strength, peace, and hope in the midst of persecution. This lesson is one that we can apply to our own lives. When we face persecution, hardship, or any kind of storm, we must remember to magnify the Lord. By doing so, we shift our perspective, build our faith, and engage in spiritual warfare. Magnifying the Lord is not just about worshiping God when things are going well; it's about praising Him in the midst of the storm, trusting that He is greater than any challenge we face. Just as David found deliverance through his praise, we too can find peace, hope, and strength by choosing to magnify the Lord in the midst of persecution.

Chapter 2 - Making God Our Refuge

In 1 Samuel 19:29 and throughout David's life, we see him constantly fleeing from King Saul's attempts to take his life. Saul, who had once favored David, became consumed by jealousy and anger as David's success and favor with the people grew. As a result, Saul relentlessly pursued David, seeking to kill him. For years, David was on the run, living in caves, forests, and foreign lands, never truly knowing when or where the next attack might come. Yet, during these perilous times, David didn't rely on his own strength or cunning to survive. Instead, he turned to God as his refuge, trusting Him to provide safety and deliverance. This pattern of seeking God as a refuge in the midst of persecution is evident not only in David's actions but also in his writings, such as in Psalms 34:1-4. In these verses, David declares his trust in the Lord, praising Him for His deliverance and protection. Through David's example, we learn that in our own storms and trials, we too must make God our refuge, knowing that He is our ultimate place of safety.

David's life was a constant storm, with danger seemingly lurking around every corner. King Saul's irrational hatred for David led to countless attempts on his life, forcing David into a life of hiding and uncertainty. However, in these moments of fear and danger, David didn't let his circumstances overwhelm him. Instead, he chose to place his trust in God, who he believed was in control of everything, even the storm he was enduring. In 1 Samuel 19:29 and the surrounding chapters, we see Saul's increasing determination to kill David, but we also see David's unwavering trust in God. Whether he was hiding in a cave or fleeing into the wilderness, David consistently turned to God for protection, seeking His guidance and trusting in His plan. This teaches us a vital lesson: in the storms of life, we must not rely solely on our own strength or strategies but, like David, make God our refuge. He is the only one who can truly protect us and provide the safety we need when the world feels threatening.

The concept of God being a refuge is one that David repeatedly emphasizes in the Psalms. In Psalm 34, David writes about his personal experiences of calling on the Lord and finding refuge in Him. He begins the Psalm by praising God, saying, "I will bless the Lord at all times: his praise shall continually be in my mouth" (Psalm 34:1). Even though David was being hunted by Saul and his life was in constant danger, he was able to praise God because he had made God his refuge. David knew that no matter how dangerous his circumstances were, God was his ultimate protector. This is why he could say in Psalm 34:4, "I sought the Lord, and he heard me, and delivered me from all my fears". By making God his refuge, David found peace and safety in the midst of the storm, and this peace came not from his surroundings but from his faith in God's ability to protect and deliver him.

David's trust in God as his refuge was not a passive or theoretical concept; it was a deeply personal and active choice. Throughout his life, David continually sought God in prayer, asking for guidance, protection, and deliverance. Even when he had opportunities to take matters into his own hands, such as when he had the chance to kill Saul in a cave (1 Samuel 24), David chose to trust in God's timing and plan. He refused to harm Saul, recognizing that God was his true refuge and deliverer, and that it was God's responsibility to deal with Saul, not his own. This teaches us an important lesson about what it means to make God our refuge. It's not just about asking for protection in times of danger; it's about trusting God's plan and timing, even when we don't understand why the storm is happening or how long it will last. David could have easily taken shortcuts to end his persecution, but he chose to wait on God, knowing that his safety and future were in God's hands.

Making God our refuge, as David did, means placing our complete trust in Him, even when everything around us seems to be falling apart. It means recognizing that our own abilities, resources, and plans are limited, and that only God can truly provide the safety and deliverance we need. David's life is a testament to this truth. Despite the many dangers he faced, David was never captured or killed by Saul, not because of his own strength or cleverness, but because God was his refuge. Time and time again, God protected David, delivering him from Saul's attempts to kill him and guiding him through the wilderness and dangerous territories. This teaches us that when we make God our refuge, we can trust that He will protect us, even when the storm seems overwhelming. It doesn't mean that we won't face difficulties or persecution, but it does mean that we can find peace and safety in God, knowing that He is in control and that His plans for us are good.

One of the key lessons we learn from David's life is that making God our refuge requires humility. David, despite being a mighty warrior and a man of great abilities, knew that he could not survive on his own. He knew that his strength and skill were not enough to protect him from Saul's relentless pursuit. In recognizing his own limitations, David humbled himself before God, acknowledging that only God could save him. This humility is essential for us as well. When we face storms and trials, it's easy to fall into the trap of thinking that we can handle everything on our own. But like David, we must recognize that we need God's protection and guidance. Making God our refuge means surrendering our pride and admitting that we cannot navigate life's storms without Him.

David's example also teaches us that making God our refuge is a daily choice. It's not something we do once and then forget about; it's a continual process of turning to God in every situation, seeking His guidance, and trusting Him with our lives. David didn't just turn to God when things were going well or when he felt strong; he turned to God in his weakest and most vulnerable moments. When he was hiding in caves, surrounded by enemies, or betrayed by those he trusted, David sought refuge in God. This is a powerful lesson for us. In the storms of life, we must make the conscious decision to turn to God, not just when it's easy or convenient, but especially when we feel overwhelmed, afraid, or uncertain.

Making God our refuge also means trusting in His promises. David clung to the promises God had made to him, knowing that God had anointed him to be the future king of Israel. Even when Saul's pursuit made it seem like that promise would never be fulfilled, David continued to trust in God's word. He knew that God was faithful and that His promises would come to pass, no matter how dire the circumstances seemed. This teaches us that when we make God our refuge, we must also hold on to His promises. Even when the storms of life make it seem like those promises are far from being fulfilled, we can trust that God is faithful and that He will bring His plans for us to completion in His perfect timing.

David's life also shows us that making God our refuge is not about escaping from our problems or avoiding hardship. David didn't live a life free from danger or persecution simply because he trusted in God. In fact, his trust in God often led him into even greater challenges. But through it all, David found peace and safety in God, knowing that no matter what happened, God was with him. This teaches us that making God our refuge doesn't mean that we won't face difficulties or persecution. In fact, we may face even greater challenges as we follow God's path. But the difference is that when we make God our refuge, we can face those challenges with confidence, knowing that God is with us and that He will protect us and guide us through the storm.

Another important lesson from David's life is that making God our refuge brings peace, even in the midst of persecution. In Psalm 34:4, David says, "I sought the Lord, and he heard me, and delivered me from all my fears". This peace didn't come from his circumstances, which were still dangerous and uncertain, but from his trust in God. When we make God our refuge, we can experience this same peace, knowing that God is in control and that He will deliver us from our fears. David's ability to praise God in the midst of persecution shows us that even in our darkest moments, we can find peace and joy by making God our refuge.

Ultimately, making God our refuge is about trust. It's about believing that God is who He says He is and that He will do what He has promised to do. David's life is a powerful example of this kind of trust. Despite the many dangers he faced, David never stopped trusting in God's protection and provision. He knew that no matter how fierce the storm, God was with him, and that was enough. This is the lesson that we can take from David's life: when we make God our refuge, we can face any storm with confidence, knowing that He is our ultimate place of safety. We may not always understand why the storm is happening, but we can trust that God is in control and that He will see us through. Just as God protected David from Saul's relentless pursuit, He will protect us and guide us through the storms of life.

In conclusion, 1 Samuel 19:29 and David's life teach us the importance of making God our refuge in the midst of persecution and trials. David's ability to find peace and safety in God, despite being constantly pursued by King Saul, shows us that no matter how dangerous or uncertain our circumstances may be, we can trust in God's protection. Making God

our refuge is not just about asking for protection; it's about trusting in His plan, surrendering our pride, and seeking His guidance in every situation. It's a daily choice to turn to God, especially when we feel overwhelmed or afraid. By making God our refuge, we can experience peace and safety, knowing that He is with us and that He will deliver us from our fears. David's life is a powerful reminder that when we make God our refuge, we can face any storm with confidence, trusting that He is our ultimate place of safety.

Chapter 3 - Maintaining Faith

In Psalm 34:4, David proclaims, "I sought the Lord, and he heard me, and delivered me from all my fears," a powerful declaration of faith that resonates through the trials and storms of his life. David's experience, as recorded in this verse, teaches us a profound lesson about maintaining faith during times of persecution, uncertainty, and hardship. Maintaining faith, especially when everything around us feels chaotic or when we are in the midst of suffering, can be one of the most challenging aspects of our spiritual journey. Yet, David's life serves as a testament to the strength that comes from trusting in God, believing that He hears us even when we can't see immediate answers. David's ability to maintain his faith, despite the relentless pursuit by King Saul, the betrayal by those close to him, and the overwhelming obstacles he faced, reminds us that faith is not about the absence of difficulties, but about trusting in God's presence and deliverance through them.

David's statement in Psalm 34:4 reflects his unwavering belief that God was always listening, even when the storms raged around him. This belief did not come easily or without struggle—David often found himself in situations where fear and doubt could have easily overtaken him. In 1 Samuel 19, we see David fleeing from Saul, unsure of where his next refuge might be, living in caves and relying on God to guide him day by day. Despite these trials, David maintained his faith by continually seeking the Lord. He didn't allow fear to paralyze him, nor did he allow doubt to distance him from God. Instead, David actively sought the Lord in prayer, worship, and praise, confident that God was not only hearing him but would deliver him in His perfect time. This teaches us that maintaining faith is not passive—it is an active, ongoing decision to seek God in the midst of hardship, to lay our fears before Him, and to trust that He is listening, even when we don't see immediate results.

One of the most important lessons we learn from David's life is that faith is not dependent on our circumstances. David's life was full of storms—literal and figurative ones. Whether he was fleeing from King Saul, battling the Philistines, or facing personal failures, David's life was marked by constant challenges. Yet, in Psalm 34:4, we see that David's faith remained unshaken because it was not rooted in his circumstances but in God's character. He believed that God was good, faithful, and just, and that belief sustained him through the darkest moments of his life. David's ability to maintain faith during persecution reminds us that our faith should not be based on how smoothly life is going, but on the unchanging nature of God. Even when everything seems to be falling apart, we can trust that God is still in control and that He hears our cries for help.

David's life also teaches us that maintaining faith doesn't mean we won't experience fear or doubt. In Psalm 34:4, David acknowledges that he had fears, but he also testifies that God delivered him from those fears. This is an important distinction—having faith doesn't mean we are never afraid or anxious; it means that we take those fears to God and trust Him to deliver us from them. David didn't deny his fear, but he refused to let it control him. Instead, he sought the Lord, trusting that God would hear him and deliver him from whatever was causing his fear. This teaches us that maintaining faith doesn't mean we won't have moments of doubt or fear, but it does mean that we don't allow those moments to define us. Like David, we can bring our fears to God, trusting that He will hear us and help us overcome them in His perfect time.

Maintaining faith during trials also requires patience. David's life is a testament to the importance of waiting on God's timing. Throughout his years of running from Saul, David had multiple opportunities to take matters into his own hands, to try and end his persecution by killing Saul or by making decisions out of fear and desperation. Yet, time and time again, David chose to wait on God. He believed that God's timing was perfect, even when it didn't align with his own desires for immediate relief. This is a powerful lesson for us. When we are in the midst of a storm, it's natural to want immediate answers or solutions. We want the pain to end, the problem to be resolved, or the fear to go away. But maintaining faith means trusting that God's timing is better than our own. It means believing that even when we don't understand why we are still in the storm, God is working things out for our good and for His glory. David's patience and trust in God's timing show us that deliverance often doesn't come immediately, but it does come when we continue to seek God and trust in His plan.

Another key aspect of maintaining faith, as seen in David's life, is the importance of praising God in the midst of trials. Psalm 34:1 says, "I will bless the Lord at all times: his praise shall continually be in my mouth." Even when David was fleeing for his life, he made the choice to praise God. This act of praise, even in the darkest moments, helped him to maintain his faith. Praising God during trials is a way of reminding ourselves of His goodness and faithfulness. It shifts our focus from the magnitude of our problems to the greatness of our God. David understood that praise was not just something to be done when things were going well, but especially when things were hard. In doing so, he kept his faith alive and strong, despite the persecution he faced. This teaches us that one of the most powerful ways to maintain our faith during trials is through praise. When we choose to praise God, even when we don't feel like it, we are declaring that we trust Him, that we believe He is good, and that we know He will deliver us.

David's ability to maintain faith also shows us the importance of remembering God's past faithfulness. Throughout his life, David faced countless storms, but each time, he could look back and see how God had delivered him before. This gave him the confidence to trust that God would deliver him again. In Psalm 34, David is reflecting on a specific time when God delivered him, and this reflection strengthened his faith for the future. This teaches us that one of the best ways to maintain our faith during current trials is to remember how God has been faithful to us in the past. When we look back at the ways God has provided, protected, and guided us, it helps us to trust that He will continue to do so in the future. David's life reminds us that faith is often built on the foundation of remembering God's past faithfulness, which gives us the strength to trust Him in the present.

Maintaining faith also means recognizing that deliverance may not always look the way we expect. David often prayed for deliverance, and while God always answered, the way He delivered David was not always immediate or straightforward. Sometimes, David had to wait; other times, God's deliverance came in ways David might not have anticipated. But through it all, David maintained his faith, trusting that God knew what was best. This teaches us that maintaining faith means being open to how God chooses to deliver us. We may have a specific idea of what we want deliverance to look like, but God's ways are higher than our ways, and His plans are better than our plans. David's trust in God's wisdom and sovereignty teaches us that part of maintaining faith is being willing to accept that God's deliverance may not come in the way or the timing we expect, but it will always be what we need.

Another lesson from David's life is that maintaining faith often involves seeking God in prayer. Psalm 34:4 begins with, "I sought the Lord." David's faith was not passive; he actively sought God in every situation. When he was afraid, he prayed. When he was uncertain, he sought God's guidance. This teaches us that maintaining faith requires us to continually seek God, especially when we are in the midst of trials. Prayer is one of the most powerful tools we have for maintaining our faith because it connects us with God and allows us to pour out our fears, doubts, and concerns before Him. David's life shows us that maintaining faith means making prayer a priority, seeking God's presence and guidance in every situation, and trusting that He hears us and will deliver us.

David's life also reminds us that maintaining faith requires community. In Psalm 34:3, David invites others to "magnify the Lord" with him, calling for collective worship. Throughout his life, David surrounded himself with people who shared his faith and who supported him during his trials. This teaches us that faith is not something we maintain on our own; we need the support and encouragement of others. In times of persecution or hardship, it's easy to feel isolated and alone, but David's life reminds us that we are not meant to go through these trials by ourselves. Surrounding ourselves with a community of believers who can encourage us, pray for us, and worship with us is essential for maintaining our faith during difficult times.

Ultimately, David's life teaches us that maintaining faith is about trusting in God's character. Even when David didn't understand why he was going through certain trials or why God was allowing certain things to happen, he never lost faith in who God was. He believed that God was good, faithful, and just, even when his circumstances seemed to suggest otherwise. This unwavering belief in God's character is what allowed David to maintain his faith, no matter what storms he faced. In Psalm 34, David is praising God not because his life is easy, but because he knows that God is worthy of praise. This teaches us that maintaining faith is not about understanding everything that is happening, but about trusting that God is who He says He is and that He will do what He has promised to do.

In conclusion, Psalm 34:4 and David's life teach us the importance of maintaining faith during trials and persecution. David's ability to seek the Lord, trust in His timing, and praise Him in the midst of hardship serves as a powerful example for all of us. Maintaining faith is not about the absence of fear or doubt, but about actively seeking God, trusting in His promises, and waiting for His deliverance. It's about praising God in the storm, remembering His past faithfulness, and believing that He will hear and deliver us in His perfect time. David's life reminds us that faith is not passive—it's an active, ongoing decision to trust God, even when we don't understand what's happening. By maintaining our faith, we can face any storm with confidence, knowing that God is with us and that He will deliver us from all our fears.

Chapter 4 - Moment of Deliverance

In Psalm 34:4, David reflects on one of the most profound truths of his life: "I sought the Lord, and he heard me, and delivered me from all my fears." This verse reveals the heart of David's relationship with God—one built on trust, dependence, and the understanding that God's deliverance often comes after the storm has passed. The "moment of deliverance" that David speaks of wasn't always immediate. Many times, David had to endure long periods of suffering, fear, and uncertainty before God stepped in to deliver him. David's life was full of storms—literal and figurative—and yet, he knew that God's deliverance was certain, even if it didn't come in the way or timing that he expected. This verse teaches us a crucial lesson about God's timing and the nature of deliverance: while we often want immediate rescue from our troubles, true deliverance often comes after we've weathered the storm, once God's perfect timing has been fulfilled. In David's case, the journey of waiting on God's timing refined his faith, built his character, and deepened his dependence on God, teaching us that the storms we face in life are not just obstacles to avoid, but opportunities to grow in faith.

David's life was marked by many storms—whether it was fleeing from King Saul's relentless pursuit, dealing with personal betrayal, or navigating the consequences of his own sin. In all these situations, David sought the Lord for deliverance. However, it's important to recognize that deliverance didn't always come right away. In fact, there were times when David had to wait for years, living in caves and hiding in the wilderness, before God finally delivered him from his enemies. This teaches us a valuable lesson about waiting on God's timing. Often, we pray for deliverance and expect an immediate answer, but God's timing is perfect, and He knows when the right moment for deliverance has arrived. Just as David learned to trust God during the long periods of waiting, we too must learn to trust that God is working behind the scenes, even when we can't see the immediate results. Our storms may last longer than we anticipated, but that doesn't mean God has abandoned us. Rather, it means He is preparing us for the moment of deliverance, which will come in His perfect time.

One of the most powerful aspects of Psalm 34:4 is the fact that David doesn't just speak of deliverance from his circumstances, but deliverance from his fears. This highlights an important truth about the storms we face in life: often, the greatest storm isn't what's happening around us, but what's happening within us. Fear, anxiety, and doubt can overwhelm us during times of trial, making it difficult to see how God is at work. David experienced this firsthand. As he fled from Saul, there were undoubtedly moments when fear gripped his heart, when he wondered if he would ever escape or find peace again. Yet, in this verse, David celebrates the fact that God delivered him not only from the physical dangers he faced but from the fear that had taken hold of his heart. This teaches us that God's deliverance isn't just about changing our circumstances; it's about transforming our hearts. Even if the storm continues to rage around us, God can bring peace to our hearts, delivering us from the fear that threatens to overwhelm us.

David's reflection on God's deliverance in Psalm 34:4 also emphasizes the importance of seeking God during times of trial. David says, "I sought the Lord, and he heard me." This wasn't a passive waiting; it was an active pursuit of God's presence, guidance, and help. In the midst of his persecution, David didn't withdraw into fear or self-pity. Instead, he turned to God, seeking His wisdom and strength. This teaches us that in our own storms, we must actively seek God, trusting that He hears our cries for help. It's easy to become discouraged or to feel abandoned when we're going through difficult times, but David's life reminds us that God is always listening. When we seek Him, He hears us. However, we must also recognize that God's deliverance comes in His time, not ours. David's story is a powerful reminder that we may not always get an immediate answer to our prayers, but that doesn't mean God isn't working. Just as David continued to seek God even when the storm persisted, we too must continue to seek God, trusting that He will deliver us in His perfect time.

Another important lesson from David's life is that deliverance often comes after the storm has accomplished its purpose. The storms we face in life aren't random; they are often used by God to refine us, strengthen our faith, and draw us closer to Him. In David's case, the long years of fleeing from Saul taught him invaluable lessons about reliance on God, patience, and leadership. These experiences shaped him into the man who would one day become king. If God had delivered David immediately, he might not have developed the deep trust and dependence on God that characterized his reign as king. This teaches us that while we may want immediate deliverance from our storms, God is often using those storms to accomplish something greater in our lives. The storm may be uncomfortable, but it is shaping us, preparing us for the moment of deliverance. Just as David was prepared for kingship through his trials, we too are being prepared for the plans God has for our lives through the storms we endure.

Waiting on God's timing can be incredibly difficult, especially when the storm seems never-ending. However, David's life shows us that waiting on God is never wasted time. During his years of waiting for deliverance, David wrote many of the Psalms, developed his skills as a leader, and deepened his relationship with God. These years of waiting were not idle; they were a time of growth and preparation. This teaches us that even when we're waiting for deliverance, God is still at work. The waiting itself is part of the process of deliverance. It's in the waiting that our faith is tested and strengthened. David's ability to wait on God's timing, even when it seemed like deliverance was far off, reminds us that God's timing is always perfect. We may not understand why we have to wait, but we can trust that God is using the waiting to accomplish His purposes in our lives.

David's life also teaches us that deliverance doesn't always look the way we expect. There were times when David probably imagined that deliverance would come through a sudden victory over Saul or an immediate end to his persecution. But God's deliverance came in ways that David might not have anticipated. Sometimes, deliverance came through unexpected allies, like Jonathan, Saul's son, who helped David escape. Other times, it came through David's ability to find refuge in unlikely places. This teaches us that while we may have a specific idea of what deliverance should look like, God's ways are higher than our ways. Deliverance may not always come in the form of immediate resolution or miraculous intervention. Sometimes, it comes through God's provision of strength, peace, and endurance to carry us through the storm. David's ability to recognize God's deliverance, even when it didn't come in the way he expected, reminds us to keep our eyes open for how God is working in our lives, even when we're still in the midst of the storm.

Another important aspect of David's reflection on deliverance is the role that faith plays in the process. David didn't wait for deliverance to praise God—he praised God in the midst of the storm. Psalm 34:1 says, "I will bless the Lord at all times: his praise shall continually be in my mouth." This is a powerful declaration of faith. David chose to praise God, not because his circumstances were easy, but because he believed in God's goodness and faithfulness. This teaches us that faith is not about waiting for deliverance before we praise God; it's about praising God in the storm, trusting that He will deliver us in His time. David's ability to maintain his faith, even when deliverance seemed far off, shows us that faith is a choice. It's a decision to trust in God's character and promises, even when we can't see the outcome. By praising God in the storm, David demonstrated his confidence that deliverance would come, even if it wasn't immediate.

David's reflection on God's deliverance also highlights the importance of gratitude. When God delivered David from his fears, David didn't take it for granted. He acknowledged that it was God who had delivered him, and he praised God for it. This teaches us that when we experience deliverance, whether it's from fear, danger, or any other kind of storm, we should respond with gratitude. It's easy to forget to thank God once the storm has passed, but David's life reminds us that we should always give thanks for the ways God delivers us. Gratitude keeps us grounded in the reality of God's faithfulness and reminds us of His constant presence in our lives. By reflecting on the ways God has delivered us in the past, we can strengthen our faith for the future storms we may face.

One of the most comforting aspects of Psalm 34:4 is the reminder that God hears us. David says, "I sought the Lord, and he heard me." This is a powerful affirmation that God is always listening. Even when we feel alone or abandoned in the storm, God hears our cries for help. David's life was full of moments when he could have felt forgotten by God, but he held onto the truth that God was always listening. This teaches us that even when we don't see immediate results, we can trust that God hears us. He is not distant or indifferent to our struggles; He is a loving Father who listens to His children. Knowing that God hears us gives us the strength to keep seeking Him, even when the storm rages on.

In conclusion, Psalm 34:4 and David's life teach us powerful lessons about God's deliverance and timing. David's ability to maintain his faith, seek the Lord, and praise Him in the midst of persecution shows us that deliverance may not always come immediately, but it will come in God's perfect time. The storms we face in life are not just obstacles to overcome; they are opportunities for growth, faith, and dependence on God. By trusting in God's timing, seeking His presence, and praising Him even in the storm, we can experience the same deliverance that David did—deliverance not only from our circumstances but from the fear and anxiety that accompany them. David's life reminds us that God is always at work, even when we can't see it, and that His deliverance is always worth the wait.

Chapter 5 - Meditating on God's Goodness

In Psalms 34:1-4, we find David, a man after God's own heart, enduring intense persecution and danger as he fled from King Saul, who sought to take his life. Despite the constant threat to his safety, David's response is not to give in to fear or despair. Instead, he continually praises God, choosing to meditate on God's goodness rather than focusing on the peril that surrounded him. This passage reveals a key lesson for anyone going through storms in life—particularly those who feel as if they are being persecuted or unfairly treated. David's ability to reflect on God's goodness in the midst of his trials teaches us that meditating on God's faithfulness, love, and protection can bring peace and strength even in the most difficult times. David didn't allow the external threats of his enemies to dictate his inner state. Instead, he deliberately chose to keep his mind fixed on the goodness of God, and this decision anchored his heart, helping him to endure persecution with faith and praise. This is a lesson for all of us: when life's storms rage, and when persecution or hardship seem overwhelming, we must make the choice to meditate on God's goodness, reflecting on His faithfulness in the past and trusting in His protection for the future.

David's life was filled with turmoil from an early age, especially during his time on the run from Saul. King Saul, once a mentor and leader to David, became consumed by jealousy as David's popularity grew after his victory over Goliath. Saul's jealousy turned into a murderous pursuit that forced David into hiding, away from the comfort of home and the security of normal life. Yet, in Psalms 34:1, David declares, "I will bless the Lord at all times: his praise shall continually be in my mouth." Even though his circumstances were perilous, David refused to stop praising God. He knew that focusing on the goodness of God, rather than the threats of his enemies, was the key to maintaining his peace and trust in the Lord. This teaches us that no matter what storms we face—whether it's persecution, illness, financial struggles, or relational conflict—there is immense power in praising God and meditating on His goodness. Praise shifts our focus from our problems to the One who holds the solution. David's commitment to praising God "at all times" reminds us that our worship and gratitude toward God shouldn't depend on our circumstances but on His unchanging nature. God is good all the time, and meditating on that truth brings peace in the midst of trials.

One of the most remarkable things about David's ability to meditate on God's goodness is that it didn't come from a place of denial or ignorance. David was fully aware of the dangers he faced. He knew that Saul's men were hunting him, and he knew that at any moment, his life could be taken. But rather than dwelling on the injustice of his situation or giving in to fear, David chose to focus on what he knew to be true about God. He knew that God had delivered him before, and he trusted that God would deliver him again. This focus on God's past faithfulness allowed David to maintain hope and peace, even when the outcome of his situation was uncertain. For us, this is a crucial lesson: meditating on God's goodness doesn't mean ignoring the reality of our problems or pretending that everything is okay. It means choosing to focus on God's character and His faithfulness, even in the midst of hardship. It means reminding ourselves that God has been faithful in the past and trusting that He will continue to be faithful in the future.

Throughout the Psalms, David often reflects on the many ways God had shown His goodness and mercy to him. He recalls how God protected him as a shepherd boy when he faced lions and bears, how God gave him victory over Goliath, and how God provided for him during his time on the run. These reflections on God's goodness helped David to strengthen his faith and maintain his peace. By meditating on what God had already done, David was able to face each new trial with confidence, knowing that the same God who had delivered him before would deliver him again. This teaches us the importance of remembering and reflecting on God's faithfulness in our own lives. When we face persecution or trials, it's easy to forget the ways God has worked in the past. But like David, we must make a conscious effort to meditate on His goodness, recounting the times He has come through for us, answered our prayers, and provided for our needs. This kind of meditation builds our faith and gives us the strength to trust God in the midst of whatever storm we are facing.

David's ability to meditate on God's goodness also highlights the importance of having a heart of gratitude. Even when he was being pursued by Saul, David found reasons to thank and praise God. He didn't focus on what he didn't have or the injustice of his situation; instead, he focused on the goodness of God and all the ways God had blessed him. This attitude of gratitude was key to David's ability to maintain peace during his trials. Gratitude shifts our perspective, helping us to see our circumstances through the lens of God's goodness rather than through the lens of fear or frustration. When we take the time to thank God for His blessings, even in the midst of hardship, it changes our outlook and helps us to trust that God is still in control. David's life reminds us that gratitude is a powerful tool in maintaining our faith during times of persecution or difficulty. By choosing to focus on God's goodness and expressing gratitude for His blessings, we can find peace even when life is hard.

Meditating on God's goodness also involves focusing on His promises. David knew that God had made promises to him—promises of protection, deliverance, and a future kingship. These promises gave David hope and courage as he faced the storms in his life. In the same way, we can meditate on the promises God has given us in His Word. The Bible is filled with promises of God's love, protection, provision, and guidance, and when we meditate on these promises, they become an anchor for our souls in times of trouble. Just as David found peace by meditating on God's promises, we too can find peace by reminding ourselves of the truths found in Scripture. God's promises are a source of strength and hope, and they remind us that no matter what we are going through, God is with us, and He will see us through.

Another important aspect of meditating on God's goodness is the way it deepens our relationship with Him. David's continual praise and meditation on God's goodness weren't just about finding peace in difficult times; they were also about drawing closer to God. By reflecting on who God is and what He has done, David developed a deeper sense of intimacy with God. This closeness allowed David to trust God more fully and to rely on Him completely, even when his life was in danger. For us, meditating on God's goodness has the same effect. When we take the time to reflect on God's faithfulness, love, and mercy, we draw closer to Him. This deepened relationship gives us the strength to endure trials and the confidence to trust in His plan, even when we don't understand what is happening.

David's life also teaches us that meditating on God's goodness can help us overcome fear. In Psalm 34:4, David says, "I sought the Lord, and he heard me, and delivered me from all my fears." David didn't pretend that he wasn't afraid; instead, he brought his fears to God and trusted that God would deliver him. By meditating on God's goodness and reflecting on His faithfulness, David was able to overcome the fear that could have easily paralyzed him. This is a powerful lesson for us. When we face fear—whether it's fear of persecution, fear of failure, or fear of the unknown—we can bring those fears to God and trust that He will deliver us. Meditating on God's goodness helps us to see our fears in the light of His power and faithfulness, reminding us that God is greater than any fear we may face.

One of the most powerful aspects of meditating on God's goodness is the peace it brings. In Philippians 4:6-7, we are told to bring our requests to God with thanksgiving, and the peace of God, which surpasses all understanding, will guard our hearts and minds in Christ Jesus. David experienced this peace firsthand. Even though he was being pursued by Saul and his life was in constant danger, David found peace by meditating on God's goodness. This peace didn't come from his circumstances—it came from his relationship with God and his trust in God's faithfulness. This teaches us that peace isn't found in the absence of trials but in the presence of God. When we meditate on God's goodness and reflect on His faithfulness, we can experience a peace that transcends our circumstances. This peace guards our hearts and minds, helping us to stay focused on God rather than being consumed by fear or anxiety.

David's ability to meditate on God's goodness also highlights the importance of perspective. When we are going through trials, it's easy to become consumed by our problems and lose sight of the bigger picture. But David's life reminds us that there is always more going on than what we can see. Even when he was being pursued by Saul, David trusted that God was working behind the scenes to accomplish His purposes. This perspective allowed David to maintain hope and trust in God, even when his circumstances seemed hopeless. Meditating on God's goodness helps us to gain this same perspective. It reminds us that God is in control, that He is working for our good, and that His plans for us are greater than we can imagine. By focusing on God's goodness, we are able to rise above our circumstances and see things from a heavenly perspective.

In conclusion, Psalm 34:1-4 and David's life teach us the importance of meditating on God's goodness, especially in times of persecution and trial. Despite being pursued by Saul and facing constant danger, David chose to focus on God's faithfulness, love, and mercy. This meditation on God's goodness gave him peace, strengthened his faith, and helped him to overcome fear. David's life is a powerful reminder that when we meditate on God's goodness, we are able to find peace and strength in the midst of life's storms. By focusing on God's character and His promises, we can rise above our circumstances and trust that He will deliver us in His perfect time. Just as David found peace by meditating on God's goodness, we too can experience peace by reflecting on God's faithfulness, love, and mercy in our own lives.

Chapter 6 - Manifesting Trust in God

In Psalms 34:1-4, David provides a powerful example of manifesting trust in God, even in the face of unrelenting persecution and danger. As he writes these verses, David is not in a place of comfort or security; rather, he is on the run from King Saul, whose jealousy and desire for power have led him to seek David's life. Despite the constant threat of death, David begins this psalm with a declaration of praise: "I will bless the Lord at all times: his praise shall continually be in my mouth." This statement is remarkable given his circumstances. It reveals a heart that has chosen to trust God even when everything seems to be falling apart. David's life and words teach us that trust in God is not about waiting for the storm to pass but about praising Him in the midst of it, confident that He is in control. Manifesting trust in God means believing in His sovereignty, protection, and timing, no matter how fierce the storm may be.

David's trust in God is evident not just in his words but in his actions. Throughout his life, particularly during his years of fleeing from Saul, David had numerous opportunities to take matters into his own hands. On several occasions, David could have killed Saul and ended his persecution. However, David chose not to. Instead, he trusted that God was in control of his situation and that it was not his place to exact revenge or force God's hand. In 1 Samuel 24, for example, David spares Saul's life in a cave, even though Saul had been hunting him down. David tells his men, "The Lord forbid that I should do this thing unto my master, the Lord's anointed, to stretch forth mine hand against him, seeing he is the anointed of the Lord" (1 Samuel 24:6). This shows a deep level of trust in God's plan. David believed that God would deal with Saul in His own time and way, and that it was not David's role to take vengeance. This teaches us that manifesting trust in God means surrendering our desire to control outcomes and instead trusting in God's wisdom and timing. It means believing that God's way is always better, even when we don't understand it.

David's ability to trust God in the midst of persecution also teaches us that trust is a choice, not a feeling. There is no doubt that David experienced fear, frustration, and confusion as he fled from Saul. After all, David had been anointed as the future king of Israel, yet instead of ruling, he was living in caves and constantly on the move to avoid death. It would have been easy for David to doubt God's promises or to question whether God had forgotten about him. However, David chose to trust God despite his feelings. He chose to believe that God was still in control, even when his circumstances suggested otherwise. This is evident in Psalm 34:4, where David says, "I sought the Lord, and he heard me, and delivered me from all my fears." David acknowledges that fear was present, but he also testifies to God's faithfulness in delivering him from that fear. This teaches us that trusting God doesn't mean we won't experience fear or doubt. Rather, it means choosing to seek God and trust in His goodness, even when our emotions tell us otherwise. Trust is an act of faith, not a passive response to favorable circumstances.

David's life also teaches us that trusting God means recognizing that His protection may not always look the way we expect. Throughout his years of fleeing from Saul, David experienced many close calls, yet God protected him each time. However, this protection didn't mean that David's life was easy or free from hardship. In fact, David's trust in God often led him into difficult and dangerous situations. Yet, David knew that God's protection didn't mean the absence of storms; it meant that God would be with him through those storms. This is a critical lesson for us. When we face persecution or trials, we often expect God's protection to mean immediate deliverance or an end to our suffering. However, God's protection is not about shielding us from all difficulties but about being with us in the midst of them. David understood this, and it's why he could praise God even while being hunted by Saul. He knew that God's presence was his ultimate protection, and that as long as God was with him, he could face any storm.

Trusting God also means believing that He has a purpose for the storms we face. David's years of persecution were not wasted time. During this period, God was shaping David's character, teaching him valuable lessons about leadership, patience, and reliance on God. These lessons would later serve David well when he became king. In the same way, the storms we face in life are often used by God to refine us, to strengthen our faith, and to prepare us for the plans He has for us. Trusting God means believing that He is at work in our lives, even when we don't understand why we're going through certain trials. It means trusting that God can use even the most difficult circumstances for our good and His glory. David's life reminds us that God's ways are higher than our ways, and His plans are far greater than we can imagine.

Manifesting trust in God also requires humility. David, despite his strength and skill as a warrior, knew that he couldn't survive without God's help. He recognized that his success and safety were not the result of his own abilities but of God's protection and guidance. This humility is evident throughout David's psalms, where he repeatedly acknowledges his dependence on God. In Psalm 34:1, David says, "I will bless the Lord at all times: his praise shall continually be in my mouth." This declaration of continual praise is a testament to David's understanding that everything he had, and everything he would accomplish, was because of God's goodness and grace. Trusting God means acknowledging that we are not in control and that we need His guidance and protection. It means humbling ourselves before Him, recognizing that without Him, we are powerless. David's life teaches us that true trust in God is rooted in humility and a deep awareness of our need for Him.

David's trust in God also teaches us that trust is active, not passive. Throughout his life, David didn't just sit back and wait for God to act; he sought God in prayer, worship, and obedience. Even in the midst of persecution, David continued to seek God's guidance, and he followed God's leading, even when it was difficult. In Psalm 34:4, David says, "I sought the Lord, and he heard me, and delivered me from all my fears." David actively sought God, and this seeking led to his deliverance. This teaches us that trusting God doesn't mean doing nothing; it means actively seeking Him, praying for His guidance, and obeying His commands. Trusting God is about aligning our actions with our faith, knowing that as we seek Him, He will guide and protect us.

David's life also shows us that manifesting trust in God brings peace, even in the midst of persecution. In Psalm 34:4, David speaks of being delivered from all his fears, even though his circumstances hadn't yet changed. This peace came not from an external change in his situation but from an internal trust in God's goodness and protection. David's trust in God allowed him to experience peace in the storm, knowing that God was with him and that He would ultimately deliver him. This teaches us that true peace is not dependent on our circumstances but on our trust in God. When we trust in His sovereignty and goodness, we can experience peace, even when the storms of life are raging around us.

Another important lesson from David's life is that trust in God produces resilience. David faced countless challenges throughout his life, from Saul's persecution to personal failures and family strife. Yet, through it all, David remained resilient because his trust was in God, not in himself or his circumstances. This resilience allowed David to endure hardship without losing hope, to keep moving forward even when the path was difficult. Trusting God gives us the strength to persevere through trials, knowing that God is in control and that He will carry us through. David's life teaches us that when we place our trust in God, we can face any storm with confidence and resilience, knowing that He is with us and that He will never leave us.

Finally, David's trust in God teaches us that deliverance comes in God's timing, not ours. Throughout his years of fleeing from Saul, David had to wait for God's deliverance. There were times when David could have taken matters into his own hands, but he chose to wait on God's timing. This teaches us that trusting God means being patient and waiting for Him to act in His perfect time. It means believing that God's timing is better than our own, even when we don't understand why we have to wait. David's life reminds us that God is never late—He always acts at the right time. Trusting Him means surrendering our timeline to His and believing that He knows what is best for us.

In conclusion, Psalms 34:1-4 and David's life provide a powerful lesson on manifesting trust in God, especially in the midst of persecution and storms. David's ability to trust God despite the constant attacks from King Saul teaches us that true trust is not about having perfect circumstances but about believing that God is in control, even when life feels chaotic. Trusting God means surrendering our desire for control, seeking Him in prayer, and relying on His protection and guidance. It means choosing to praise Him, even when the storm is raging, and believing that His timing is perfect.

Chapter 7 - Measuring Strength in God

David's life, filled with many storms and challenges, offers valuable lessons on how to respond when life feels overwhelming, particularly in Psalm 34:1-4. One of the most significant lessons David teaches us through these verses is that true strength comes not from focusing on our enemies or the problems we face, but from turning our hearts to God in praise. In Psalm 34:1, David declares, "I will bless the Lord at all times: his praise shall continually be in my mouth," showing us that even in the darkest moments of his life, he made the conscious decision to bless and praise God. This choice to praise God, no matter the situation, reveals a key truth about how we should handle difficult times. Often, when storms come into our lives, we tend to focus on the problems, letting fear and anxiety take over. David, however, teaches us the opposite. Rather than dwelling on the danger he faced while being pursued by King Saul or allowing himself to be consumed by the persecution that surrounded him, he directed his focus upward, towards God. This shift in perspective is powerful. It reminds us that praising God, even when everything seems to be falling apart, allows us to tap into a strength greater than our own. David understood that his strength did not come from his own abilities or from his circumstances, but from the Lord. This is a crucial lesson for us: when we are faced with trials, instead of measuring our strength by what we can do, we should measure it by God's power, which is infinite and unchanging. In Psalm 34:2, David continues, "My soul shall make her boast in the Lord: the humble shall hear thereof, and be glad." This verse reminds us that when we humble ourselves before God, acknowledging that we cannot face our challenges alone, we find joy and strength. Boasting in the Lord means recognizing that He is our source of help, protection, and deliverance. When we focus on God's greatness and His ability to carry us through our storms, it lifts our spirits and gives us hope. David's humility in praising God also serves as an example for others. When we choose to praise God in the midst of our struggles, it not only strengthens our faith but can also inspire and encourage those around us. This is why David says in Psalm 34:3, "O magnify the Lord with me, and let us exalt his name together." David invites others to join him in praising God, showing that worship can be a communal experience that brings people together in faith. When we come together to praise God, especially in difficult times, it reminds us that we are not alone in our struggles and that God's power is greater than anything we face. The fourth verse, Psalm 34:4, reveals the result of David's trust in God: "I sought the Lord, and he heard me, and delivered me from all my fears." This verse demonstrates God's faithfulness to those who seek Him. When David cried out to God in his distress, God not only heard him but delivered him from the fears that had gripped his heart. This shows us that God is not distant or uncaring during our storms; rather, He is ready and willing to come to our aid when we call on Him. The lesson here is clear: when we turn to God in prayer and praise, even when we are afraid or in danger, God listens and provides the strength and peace we need to face our fears. David's experience of being delivered from his fears is a powerful reminder for us that God can do the same in our lives. No matter what storm we are going through—whether it is persecution, fear, or uncertainty—God is able to deliver us and give us peace if we trust in Him. Through these verses, David teaches us that the key to overcoming our storms is not by focusing on the size of the storm but by focusing on the greatness of our God. We must measure our strength by God's power, not by our circumstances. When we do this, we can face any challenge with confidence, knowing that God is with us, that He hears us, and that He will deliver us from all our fears. This lesson from David's storms is one that we can carry with us throughout our lives, trusting that no matter what we face, God is greater, and His power is enough to see us through. By praising God in the midst of our storms, like David did, we can experience the peace and strength that only comes from Him, allowing us to rise above our circumstances and find hope, even in the darkest of times.

Chapter 8 - Mourning with Hope

David, a man after God's own heart, faced many storms in his life, especially during times of persecution. In Psalm 34:1-4, we see how David responded to these challenges, not by denying his pain or pretending that his struggles didn't affect him, but by mourning with hope in God's deliverance. This passage teaches us that it's natural to feel sorrow in the midst of trials, but it also shows us the importance of balancing that sorrow with hope in God's mercy and rescue. David's life was marked by intense periods of persecution, whether it was King Saul relentlessly pursuing him or enemies seeking to destroy him, yet in the midst of all this, David didn't allow despair to take root in his heart. Instead, he brought his laments to God, pouring out his heart while holding onto the belief that God would hear him and bring him through the storm. This mixture of mourning and hope is central to the lesson David teaches us. In Psalm 34:1, David begins with a powerful declaration: "I will bless the Lord at all times: his praise shall continually be in my mouth." This statement reveals David's mindset, even in the face of hardship. While he mourned the suffering he endured, he also chose to focus on God's goodness and faithfulness. By praising God continuously, David reminded himself of who God is—a loving, merciful, and all-powerful Savior. This teaches us that, while it is human to feel sorrow, we should never lose sight of God's ability to rescue us. Even when the storms of life seem overwhelming, we can still find a reason to bless the Lord because we know that He is in control and will ultimately deliver us. In the next verse, Psalm 34:2, David writes, "My soul shall make her boast in the Lord: the humble shall hear thereof, and be glad." Here, David is acknowledging that his confidence and hope are not in his own strength or in the circumstances changing immediately, but in the Lord. David's mourning was filled with humility, recognizing that he couldn't overcome his challenges on his own. Instead, he trusted in God's mercy and power. This verse teaches us that true hope is found in humbly surrendering our struggles to God, knowing that He is able to lift us up. It's okay to mourn, to feel the weight of the trials we face, but we should do so with the understanding that God is our refuge and strength. When we boast in the Lord, we remind ourselves and others that God is faithful and that our hope is not misplaced. David's mourning wasn't without hope because he knew that God was with him, guiding him through the storms of life. Psalm 34:3 goes on to say, "O magnify the Lord with me, and let us exalt his name together." David invites others to join him in praising God, even in the midst of trials. This shows us that mourning with hope is not just a personal experience, but something we can share with others. When we come together to magnify the Lord, we remind each other of God's goodness and encourage one another to keep trusting in His deliverance. David's call to exalt God's name together also teaches us that our hope in God's mercy can be a source of encouragement for those around us. When others see us praising God, even in difficult times, it can inspire them to hold onto hope as well. Mourning with hope, as David did, is not about ignoring our pain, but about choosing to focus on God's ability to bring us through it. In Psalm 34:4, David shares the result of his hope-filled mourning: "I sought the Lord, and he heard me, and delivered me from all my fears." This verse is a beautiful reminder that when we bring our sorrows and fears to God, He listens and responds. David didn't just cry out in despair; he cried out with the hope that God would hear him and act. And God did. David's testimony of being delivered from his fears is a powerful example of how mourning with hope leads to God's rescue. This doesn't mean that the storms will immediately cease, but it does mean that God will provide the strength, peace, and comfort we need to endure them. David's story shows us that it's okay to grieve our trials, to feel the weight of persecution and hardship, but we must do so with the hope that God is faithful to deliver us. His mercy is always present, even when we can't see it right away. The lesson from David's storms is that mourning is a natural response to the challenges we face, but it should always be paired with hope in God's mercy. When we approach our trials with this balance, we open ourselves up to experience God's deliverance in ways we never thought possible. David's example teaches us that no matter how difficult life gets, we can still find hope in the Lord. We can mourn the loss, the pain, and the suffering we face, but we do so knowing that God hears our cries and will deliver us. This hope allows us to endure the storms, not with despair, but with the confidence that God is working on our behalf. Mourning with hope, as David did, transforms our perspective. It allows us to acknowledge the reality of our pain without being overwhelmed by it. Instead, we place our trust in God, believing that His mercy will see us through. David's life shows us that even in the darkest moments, we can find hope by praising God and seeking His deliverance. As we face our own storms, we can learn from David's example and choose to mourn with hope, trusting in God's mercy and faithfulness to bring us through.

Chapter 9 - Moving Forward with Praise

David's life, as portrayed in the Bible, is a testament to perseverance in the face of danger and hardship, and Psalm 34:1-4 captures an important lesson about how we, too, should continue moving forward with praise in our hearts, even when life feels overwhelming. In Psalm 34:1, David declares, "I will bless the Lord at all times: his praise shall continually be in my mouth." This statement reflects his unwavering commitment to praise God no matter what he faced. David's life was marked by numerous storms, from being hunted by King Saul to facing betrayal, danger, and moments of intense personal despair, yet in the midst of it all, David never stopped praising God. He understood that his mission to serve God did not pause when life got tough. Rather than allowing the hardships to paralyze him, David chose to press on with praise as his guide. This teaches us a profound lesson: when we face our own storms—whether they come in the form of danger, loss, or trials—we are called to keep moving forward, trusting in God's faithfulness and power. Psalm 34:1 reminds us that praise should not be reserved for moments of peace or success, but that it must continue even when we are walking through life's most challenging storms. David's praise was not just a passive act of words, but an active choice to focus on God's greatness rather than the size of the problems he faced. By praising God, David was aligning his heart with the truth that God is bigger than any obstacle, and that even in hardship, God is worthy of all praise. This mindset of continual praise helped David stay focused on his mission to serve God, regardless of the dangers surrounding him. In our own lives, we are often tempted to stop or slow down when things get hard. We may feel overwhelmed by the challenges before us, whether they be personal struggles, health problems, or external opposition, and think that we should wait for better circumstances before we continue pursuing what God has called us to do. But David's example shows us that we don't have to wait for the storm to pass in order to keep moving forward. In fact, it is precisely in those moments of danger and difficulty that our praise becomes even more powerful and meaningful. When we choose to praise God in the midst of a storm, we are declaring our trust in Him, acknowledging that He is in control and that He will carry us through. This is why David continues in Psalm 34:2, saying, "My soul shall make her boast in the Lord: the humble shall hear thereof, and be glad." David wasn't boasting in his own ability to overcome the challenges he faced; he was boasting in the Lord. He recognized that his strength, his protection, and his ability to keep moving forward all came from God. This is another key lesson for us: when we praise God, we are not relying on our own strength to get through life's storms. Instead, we are boasting in the Lord's strength and trusting that He will provide what we need to keep going. David's humility in this verse shows us the importance of acknowledging that we cannot do it alone. We need God's help, and when we humble ourselves before Him, He gives us the strength to continue our journey, no matter how difficult it may seem. David's life was a continuous mission to serve God, and even when danger was imminent, he didn't stop moving forward. He didn't let fear or hardship hold him back from what he knew God had called him to do. Instead, he chose to magnify the Lord, as he says in Psalm 34:3, "O magnify the Lord with me, and let us exalt his name together." This verse is a powerful reminder that our praise can inspire others to join us in worshiping God, even in the midst of their own storms. David invites others to come alongside him and magnify the Lord together, showing that praise is not just a personal act, but something that can unite and strengthen a community of believers. When we continue to praise God while we face trials, we become a testimony to others that God is worthy of praise, no matter the circumstances. Our perseverance through praise can encourage others to do the same, and together, we can lift up God's name and declare His goodness, even in the most difficult seasons of life. In Psalm 34:4, David shares the result of his decision to seek God and praise Him despite the danger: "I sought the Lord, and he heard me, and delivered me from all my fears." This verse reminds us that God is not distant or unaware of our struggles. When we seek Him, He hears us, and He delivers us from our fears. David's continual praise in the face of danger wasn't in vain. God responded to David's faith and trust, delivering him from the very fears that threatened to overwhelm him. This shows us that when we keep moving forward with praise, we are not just going through the motions; we are actively inviting God's presence and deliverance into our situation. God honors our faith when we choose to praise Him, even when life is hard, and He promises to be with us, delivering us from fear and giving us the strength to keep going. The lesson from David's life is clear: no matter what danger or storm we face, we can keep moving forward by continually praising God. Praise is not just a response to good times; it is a declaration of our trust in God's faithfulness, even in the hardest moments. As we walk through life's storms, we must remember that our strength comes from the Lord, and that by praising Him, we align our hearts with His power and protection. Like David, we can choose to keep moving forward with praise, knowing that God is with us and that He will see us through every challenge.

Chapter 10 - Mercy in the Midst of Trials

David's life, especially during the time he was fleeing from King Saul, provides a powerful example of how God's mercy is present even in the midst of our greatest trials. In Psalm 34:1-4, David reflects on his experiences of persecution and danger, and through his words, we learn a vital lesson: even when we are surrounded by difficulties, God's mercy is never far away. David's storms were not small or insignificant. He was being hunted, his life was at risk, and he faced betrayal and hardship at every turn. Yet, in the middle of these trials, David continually experienced God's mercy in ways that strengthened his faith and kept him moving forward. Psalm 34:1 begins with David's declaration: "I will bless the Lord at all times: his praise shall continually be in my mouth." This shows us that, despite the immense challenges he faced, David chose to praise God. He didn't wait for his situation to improve before acknowledging God's goodness; instead, he praised God in the very middle of his trials. Why? Because David knew that God's mercy was still at work, even when life felt overwhelming. This teaches us that we, too, can bless the Lord during our hardest moments, trusting that His mercy is sustaining us even when we can't see it clearly. David understood that God's mercy isn't something that disappears when we're in trouble. In fact, it often becomes more evident during those times. By praising God at all times, David was acknowledging that God's mercy was still active, guiding him, protecting him, and providing for him in ways that went beyond what was immediately visible. For David, God's mercy was not a distant or abstract concept; it was a daily reality. This is a key lesson for us: when we face trials, we should not only look for the obvious signs of God's intervention but also recognize the quiet, steady ways His mercy is carrying us through. In Psalm 34:2, David continues, "My soul shall make her boast in the Lord: the humble shall hear thereof, and be glad." Here, David shows us the connection between humility and experiencing God's mercy. David wasn't boasting in his own ability to survive the trials he faced; he was boasting in the Lord's mercy, which was the true source of his strength and deliverance. This humility is essential because it opens the door for us to recognize and receive God's mercy. When we humble ourselves, acknowledging that we can't get through our trials on our own, we create space for God's mercy to work in our lives. David's life is filled with moments where, despite the danger he was in, God showed up in unexpected ways, providing mercy and protection. Whether it was through the kindness of strangers, the loyalty of his friends, or even the natural world around him, David experienced God's mercy in countless ways. This is a reminder to us that, even when life feels out of control, God's mercy is always present, often working behind the scenes to protect and guide us. Psalm 34:3 further emphasizes the importance of recognizing God's mercy in our lives: "O magnify the Lord with me, and let us exalt his name together." David invites others to join him in praising God, showing that experiencing God's mercy is not just a personal experience but something that can be shared and celebrated with others. When we recognize God's mercy in the midst of our trials, it strengthens our faith and encourages those around us. David's life was a testimony to the fact that God's mercy is always at work, even when things seem darkest. By praising God and sharing his experiences of mercy, David inspired others to trust in God's faithfulness, even in their own times of trial. This shows us that our trials can become opportunities to magnify the Lord and declare His mercy to those around us. When we share how God has shown us mercy in our hardest times, it encourages others to look for His mercy in their own lives. In Psalm 34:4, David sums up his experience with these words: "I sought the Lord, and he heard me, and delivered me from all my fears." This verse is a powerful reminder that God's mercy is not only present during our trials, but it also brings deliverance. David sought the Lord in the midst of his fears, and God, in His mercy, heard him and delivered him. This doesn't mean that David's trials disappeared immediately, but it does mean that God gave him the strength and peace he needed to continue. David's story shows us that God's mercy often comes in the form of inner peace and strength, enabling us to face our fears and continue moving forward, even when the storm is still raging. God's mercy is not just about removing our problems; it's about giving us what we need to endure them and ultimately come out stronger on the other side. The lesson from David's life is clear: even in the midst of our greatest trials, we can expect to experience God's mercy. His mercy is not limited by our circumstances, nor is it dependent on everything going smoothly in our lives. In fact, it is often during our hardest moments that God's mercy becomes most evident. Like David, we can seek the Lord, knowing that He hears us and will deliver us from our fears in His perfect timing. This gives us hope and assurance that no matter how difficult our trials may be, we are never beyond the reach of God's mercy. David's life is a testament to the fact that God's mercy is always present, even when we're running from danger, facing persecution, or feeling overwhelmed by life's challenges. As we walk through our own trials, we can take comfort in the knowledge that God's mercy is with us every step of the way. By following David's example—praising God in the midst of our trials, humbling ourselves before Him, and seeking His deliverance—we can experience the peace and strength that come from knowing that God's mercy is greater than any storm we face.

Chapter 11 - Multiplying God's Praise

David's declaration in Psalm 34:1, "I will bless the Lord at all times: his praise shall continually be in my mouth," is a powerful reminder of the importance of praising God in every season, especially during persecution and trials. This verse teaches us a crucial lesson about multiplying our praise to God, lifting Him higher through every challenge we face. David, a man who experienced relentless persecution, teaches us that even in the midst of our greatest struggles, we must commit ourselves to praising God without ceasing. His life was filled with storms—he was constantly on the run from King Saul, faced betrayal, and dealt with intense personal hardships—yet David made the conscious decision to bless the Lord at all times. This wasn't a statement made during a time of ease or comfort, but one spoken in the midst of danger and uncertainty. The key lesson here is that our praise should not be dependent on our circumstances. Instead, we are called to multiply our praise, giving God glory through every situation, no matter how difficult it may seem.

David's decision to bless the Lord continually is an act of spiritual maturity and faith. It teaches us that in times of persecution, when life feels overwhelming and we are tempted to focus on our problems, we should instead focus on praising God. By doing this, we are lifting God higher than our circumstances, acknowledging that His power and goodness are greater than any trial we might face. Multiplying our praise means that we don't just praise God in the good times, but we increase our praise in the difficult moments. This is what David did, and it's what we are called to do as well. When we face trials, it can be easy to let fear, anxiety, and doubt take over. But by multiplying our praise, we shift our focus from the size of our problems to the greatness of our God.

In Psalm 34:2, David continues, "My soul shall make her boast in the Lord: the humble shall hear thereof, and be glad." Here, David is showing us that boasting in the Lord—lifting God higher and higher through our praise—brings joy not only to ourselves but to others who witness our faith. This is a vital aspect of multiplying praise. When we lift God up in the middle of our storms, it doesn't just strengthen our own hearts; it encourages those around us. The humble, those who are also going through difficult times, will hear our praise and be glad. They will be reminded that God is still worthy of praise, no matter what they are going through. This creates a ripple effect, where our praise inspires others to do the same, multiplying God's praise even further. This is a beautiful picture of how praise works in the life of a believer. It's not just about lifting our own spirits; it's about multiplying that praise in such a way that it impacts the people around us, drawing them closer to God and encouraging them to lift their eyes to Him as well.

David's life shows us that when we multiply our praise, it has the power to change our perspective. In Psalm 34:3, David invites others to join him in this multiplied praise: "O magnify the Lord with me, and let us exalt his name together." This invitation to magnify the Lord is a call to focus on God's greatness rather than the problems that surround us. When we magnify something, we make it appear larger in our vision. By magnifying the Lord, we are choosing to make God bigger in our minds and hearts than the difficulties we face. This is the essence of multiplying praise—making a deliberate decision to lift God higher and higher in our thoughts and actions, especially during times of trial. David knew that in the face of persecution, the best thing he could do was to make God the focus of his life, not his troubles. By doing so, he was able to maintain his faith and trust in God's deliverance. And by inviting others to join him in this act of magnifying God, David was encouraging a community of believers to do the same, thus multiplying the praise of God even more.

Psalm 34:4 reveals the result of this multiplied praise: "I sought the Lord, and he heard me, and delivered me from all my fears." David's act of continually praising God, even in the midst of persecution, led to his deliverance. This is a key lesson for us. When we choose to multiply our praise, seeking God and lifting Him higher, we open the door for His deliverance in our lives. David didn't wait for his circumstances to improve before he praised God; he praised God in the middle of his storm, and in response, God delivered him from his fears. This shows us that multiplied praise is not just about enduring trials; it's about inviting God's power and presence into those trials. When we lift God higher through our praise, we remind ourselves that He is in control, and we invite His intervention into our situation. David's story teaches us that multiplied praise has the power to break the chains of fear and deliver us from the things that hold us back.

Moreover, David's life reminds us that multiplied praise is a choice we make in every season of life, especially in the hard times. It's easy to praise God when everything is going well, but the true test of our faith comes when we are in the midst of persecution, hardship, or fear. This is where multiplied praise becomes so important. It's in these moments that we have to choose to bless the Lord at all times, just as David did. By making this choice, we are demonstrating our trust in God's sovereignty and goodness. We are saying that we believe God is worthy of praise, not because our circumstances are perfect, but because He is perfect. And as we continue to lift God higher through our praise, we find that our faith is strengthened, our perspective is changed, and our fears begin to fade in the light of God's greatness.

The lesson from Psalm 34:1-4 is clear: we are called to multiply our praise, lifting God higher in every season of life, especially during persecution and trials. David's example shows us that praise is not just a reaction to good times; it's a weapon we use to fight through the hard times. By choosing to bless the Lord at all times, we align ourselves with God's power and invite His deliverance into our lives. When we multiply our praise, we also inspire others to do the same, creating a ripple effect that spreads God's glory even further. In the end, multiplying our praise is not just about surviving the storm; it's about thriving in the storm by lifting God higher and trusting that He will bring us through. David's life is a testament to the power of multiplied praise, and as we follow his example, we too can experience the peace, strength, and deliverance that come from lifting God higher in every season of life.

Chapter 12 - Mastering the Art of Gratitude

David's life, as captured in the Bible, teaches us profound lessons about how to respond to life's storms, especially the value of gratitude in the face of persecution. In Psalm 34:1-4, we see a beautiful example of how David, despite being pursued by enemies and facing incredible trials, consistently chose gratitude as his response. His declaration, "I will bless the Lord at all times: his praise shall continually be in my mouth," is a powerful reminder that gratitude and praise should not be limited to times of peace and prosperity. Instead, David shows us that mastering the art of gratitude, even in the midst of suffering, is what allows us to rise above our circumstances and focus on God's goodness and provision. This mindset is not only a form of worship but a way of protecting our hearts and minds from becoming overwhelmed by the hardships we face.

David's life was filled with intense storms—whether it was running from King Saul, dealing with betrayal from those close to him, or facing the consequences of his own mistakes—yet throughout these trials, he made a conscious decision to remain grateful. This teaches us that gratitude is not an automatic response to hardship; it's something we must intentionally cultivate, just as David did. By mastering gratitude, David was able to focus not on the difficulties around him, but on the blessings and provision of God. In Psalm 34:1, when David says he will bless the Lord at all times, he is showing us that gratitude is a choice, a decision to focus on what God has done rather than what is going wrong. This is the foundation of mastering gratitude: understanding that no matter how dark the storm, there is always something to thank God for.

David's choice to continually praise God, even in the midst of his persecution, was not just a personal act of worship, but a powerful testimony of faith. His life shows us that gratitude in difficult times is not only for our own benefit, but it also serves as a witness to others about the faithfulness of God. When David proclaimed, "My soul shall make her boast in the Lord: the humble shall hear thereof, and be glad," in Psalm 34:2, he was expressing the idea that his gratitude would inspire others to see the goodness of God. This teaches us that when we master the art of gratitude, we are not only lifting our own spirits, but we are also encouraging those around us who may be going through their own storms. Gratitude has the power to multiply, and as we choose to focus on God's blessings in our lives, others will see our example and be encouraged to do the same.

Mastering gratitude, as David did, also requires a shift in perspective. It's easy to be grateful when everything is going well, but true gratitude is developed in the storm. David's life demonstrates that gratitude is not about denying the existence of problems or pretending that everything is perfect; rather, it's about recognizing that even in the midst of persecution and trials, God is still providing for us, protecting us, and working on our behalf. Psalm 34:3 says, "O magnify the Lord with me, and let us exalt his name together." This invitation to magnify the Lord is a call to focus on the greatness of God, even when our problems seem overwhelming. When we magnify God, we make Him bigger in our hearts and minds, which helps us to put our challenges in perspective. Gratitude allows us to do this—it shifts our focus from the size of the storm to the greatness of God's provision. David mastered this art of gratitude by continually lifting his eyes to God and praising Him for His faithfulness, even when his circumstances were far from ideal.

In Psalm 34:4, David gives us a glimpse into the result of mastering gratitude: "I sought the Lord, and he heard me, and delivered me from all my fears." This verse reveals that gratitude opens the door to God's deliverance. When David sought the Lord in gratitude and praise, God responded by delivering him from his fears. This teaches us that gratitude is not just a nice thing to do; it is a powerful spiritual practice that invites God's presence and intervention into our lives. By choosing gratitude, we are aligning ourselves with God's will and demonstrating our trust in His provision, even when we can't see the full picture. Gratitude, in this sense, becomes a weapon against fear and despair. When we focus on what God has done and is doing, our fears begin to lose their power over us. David's life is a testament to the fact that mastering gratitude leads to peace, even in the midst of persecution and uncertainty.

Another key aspect of mastering gratitude is learning to see God's provision in the small things. David's life was filled with moments where God's hand was at work, even in the details. Whether it was finding refuge in a cave, receiving food from a friend, or experiencing moments of peace in the middle of chaos, David recognized that God was providing for him every step of the way. This teaches us that gratitude is not just about the big, obvious blessings; it's about recognizing the small ways that God sustains us each day. When we focus on these small blessings, we begin to see that God's provision is constant, even in the hardest times. Mastering gratitude means training ourselves to look for these moments and to thank God for them, knowing that they are evidence of His faithfulness.

David's example also shows us that mastering gratitude is not about ignoring our emotions or pretending that we don't feel pain or fear. In fact, the Psalms are filled with David's honest cries to God, expressing his frustration, fear, and sorrow. But even in the midst of these raw emotions, David always returned to a posture of gratitude. He didn't allow his circumstances to steal his praise. This teaches us that it's okay to feel pain and to mourn our losses, but we must also remember to thank God for His presence with us in those moments. Gratitude doesn't erase our problems, but it gives us the strength to face them with hope, knowing that God is with us and that He will provide what we need to get through. David mastered this balance, and it allowed him to rise above his circumstances and maintain his faith, even when life was incredibly difficult.

As we seek to master the art of gratitude in our own lives, we can learn from David's example. Gratitude is not something that comes naturally in the middle of a storm, but it is something that we can develop through intentional practice. Like David, we can choose to bless the Lord at all times, even when life is hard. We can choose to focus on the ways that God is providing for us, protecting us, and guiding us, rather than getting lost in the challenges we face. By doing this, we can rise above persecution and trials, keeping our eyes fixed on the goodness of God. Mastering gratitude allows us to see that God is always at work, even in the darkest moments, and that His provision is more than enough to sustain us.

In conclusion, David's life exemplifies the power of gratitude in the midst of storms. His ability to bless the Lord at all times, to magnify God's greatness, and to focus on the blessings of God's provision, even when he was being persecuted, teaches us that gratitude is not just a response to good times but a practice that can carry us through the hardest seasons of life. By mastering gratitude, as David did, we can rise above our circumstances, focus on God's provision, and experience His peace and deliverance. Gratitude transforms our perspective, strengthens our faith, and invites God's presence into our lives in powerful ways.

Conclusion

As we conclude "David's Song of Deliverance: Praising God Through Every Storm", we reflect on the incredible journey we've taken through the life of King David. Through trials, persecution, heartbreak, and even personal failures, David continually turned his heart to God in praise. His life was marked by moments of deep sorrow and intense battles, yet it was also characterized by unwavering faith in God's deliverance. David's psalms are a powerful reminder that no matter what storms we face, God is always present, always faithful, and always deserving of our praise.

David understood something that is vital for every believer to grasp: praise is not just for the good times; it is a lifeline in the midst of life's darkest storms. It invites God's presence, strengthens our faith, and brings peace to our souls even when the world around us is in chaos. As we've seen in David's story, praising God through trials is not just an act of worship—it is an act of spiritual warfare. It shifts our focus from the problems we face to the God who holds us in His hands. David's life teaches us that deliverance may not always come immediately, but it is certain for those who trust in the Lord.

Now, the challenge for each of us as Christians is this: Will we continue to praise God, not only in the moments of victory but also in the storms? David's life was not free of hardship, and neither will ours be. Jesus told us in John 16:33 that in this world we will face tribulation, but He also reminded us to take heart because He has overcome the world. As followers of Christ, we are called to walk by faith and not by sight, to trust that God is working in every situation, and to offer Him the sacrifice of praise even when it feels difficult.

As you continue your walk with the Lord, commit to making praise a regular part of your life. When trials come—and they will—let your first response be to lift your voice in worship, just as David did. Remember that praise is not dependent on your circumstances but on the character of God, who is unchanging, merciful, and all-powerful. By praising God through every storm, you invite His presence into your situation and position yourself to receive His peace and deliverance.

I challenge you to make Psalm 34:1 your declaration: "I will bless the Lord at all times: his praise shall continually be in my mouth." Let this be more than just words—let it be the foundation of your faith. Whether in times of joy or sorrow, abundance or need, choose to bless the Lord. Praise Him for who He is, for what He has done, and for what He has promised to do.

As you go forward, trust that the God who delivered David will deliver you. Keep praising Him, keep trusting Him, and watch as He leads you through every storm. In doing so, you will not only experience God's deliverance for yourself, but you will also inspire others to lift their eyes to the Lord and find hope in His unfailing love. Let David's song of deliverance become your song, and may you praise God through every storm you encounter.

Don't miss out!

Visit the website below and you can sign up to receive emails whenever Joshua Rhoades publishes a new book. There's no charge and no obligation.

https://books2read.com/r/B-A-AJLBB-BWOAF

BOOKS2READ

Connecting independent readers to independent writers.

Did you love *David's Song Of Deliverance Praising God Through Every Storm*? Then you should read *Anchored In Truth Exploring The Depths of Psalm 119*[1] by Joshua Rhoades!

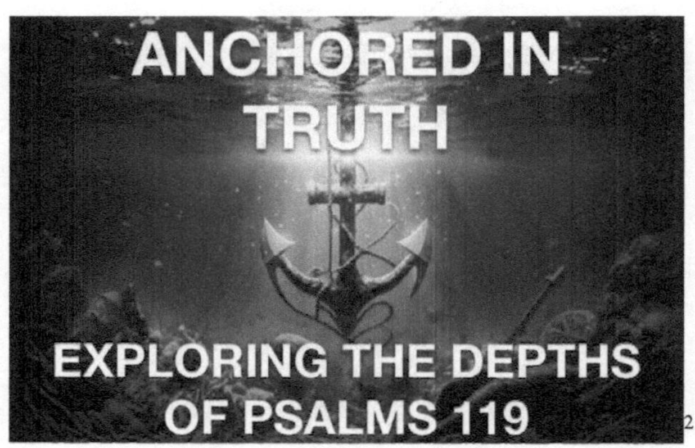

[2]

"Anchored in Truth: Exploring the Depths of Psalm 119" is an invitation to dive into one of the Bible's most profound passages, offering a deep exploration of faith, devotion, and the transformative power of God's Word. As the longest chapter in the Bible, Psalm 119 is a masterpiece of spiritual expression, structured as an intricate acrostic with each section beginning with a letter of the Hebrew alphabet. This psalm is not just a collection of verses; it is a meditation on the beauty and necessity of God's law. Through its 176 verses, the psalmist reveals a fervent love for God's commandments, a deep dependence on His guidance, and an unyielding pursuit of understanding and wisdom found only in the Scriptures.

"Anchored in Truth" invites you to explore the rich themes of Psalm 119, offering insights into how God's Word can shape, guide, and sustain a life of faith. This book is crafted not just to help you understand the words of this ancient psalm but to experience them in a way that profoundly impacts your daily walk with God. As you journey through each section, you will see how the psalmist's experiences resonate with the challenges and triumphs of your own spiritual life—whether it's seeking deliverance in trials, finding delight in God's statutes, or pleading for divine guidance.

---

1. https://books2read.com/u/mvPayX

2. https://books2read.com/u/mvPayX

This book is more than an intellectual study; it is a call to transformation. Psalm 119 urges us to anchor our lives in the unchanging truth of God's Word, making it the foundation of our character, decisions, and ultimate hope. The psalmist's devotion to God's law reminds us that Scripture is not just a set of rules or a historical text; it is the living Word of God, active and relevant in every aspect of our lives.

"Anchored in Truth" aims to inspire you to cultivate a deeper love for God's Word, seek His guidance in all things, and live out the truths found in these verses. As you read, may you be encouraged to stand firm in the faith, anchored in the unshakable truths of God's Word, and experience the wisdom, peace, and joy that come from living in alignment with His eternal commands.